FES

JESSICA ENNIS

UNAUTHORISED BIOGRAPHY

MICHAEL HURLEY

Raintree is an imprint of Capstone Global Library Limited, a company incorporated in England and Wales having its registered office at 7 Pilgrim Street, London, EC4V 6LB – Registered company number: 6695582

To contact Raintree, please phone 0845 6044371, fax + 44 (0) 1865 312263, or email myorders@raintreepublishers.co.uk.

Text © Capstone Global Library Limited 2013
First published in 2013
The moral rights of the proprietor have been asserted.

Edited by Charlotte Guillain
Designed by Philippa Jenkins
Picture research by Mica Brancic
Printed and bound in China by CTPS
 Printing Company

ISBN 978 1 406 26691 7 (hardback)
17 16 15 14 13
10 9 8 7 6 5 4 3 2 1

ISBN 978 1 406 26693 1 (paperback)
17 16 15 14 13
10 9 8 7 6 5 4 3 2 1

British Library Cataloguing in Publication Data
Hurley, Michael.
Jessica Ennis. -- (Sport files)
A full catalogue record for this book is available from the British Library.

Acknowledgements
We would like to thank the following for permission to reproduce photographs: © Photoshot/Emma Hier p.**23**; © Getty Images pp.**5**, **7**, **8**, **11** (Michael Steele), **9** (Ryan Pierse), **10** (Andy Lyons), **14** (AFP Photo/Franck Fife), **16**, **19** (adidas), **21**, **22** (Jamie Squire), **24** (WPA Pool/John Stillwell), **25** (Dave J Hogan), **26**, **27** (Ian Walton); © Getty Images for Aviva p.**17**; © Press Association/AP/David J Phillip p.**13**.

Cover photograph of Jessica Ennis reproduced with permission of © Getty Images/Michael Steele.

Every effort has been made to contact copyright holders of material reproduced in this book. Any omissions will be rectified in subsequent printings if notice is given to the publisher.

CONTENTS

Some words are printed in bold, **like this**. You can find out what they mean by looking in the glossary.

To be good at any sport, an athlete has to have some natural talent and ability. To be the best in the world takes more than just natural talent; it takes huge **sacrifice** and unending determination. A world-class athlete must also be willing to learn from experienced **coaches** who are committed to helping them become the best athlete he or she can be. In the case of Jessica Ennis, all the training and coaching has led to her becoming one of the greatest athletes in the world.

Jessica's achievements in her sport of **heptathlon** have been amazing. She has made an incredible journey from winning the bronze medal at her first major championships, the 2006 **Commonwealth Games**, to winning gold at the 2012 World Championships, to breaking the British heptathlon record in 2012, before going on to win the greatest prize in athletics: an Olympic gold medal, at the 2012 Olympic Games held in London.

FAST FACT FILE

Name:	Jessica Ennis
Born:	28 January 1986, Sheffield, England
Height:	1.65 metres (5 ft 5 inches)
Weight:	57 kilograms (125.6 pounds)
Family:	Mum Alison, dad Vinnie, sister Carmel
Favourite sports:	Tennis and gymnastics
Favourite food:	Italian
Favourite number:	19
Favourite types of music:	R'n'B, hip-hop

Jessica has overcome disappointment, injury, and immense pressure to achieve her dream of becoming an Olympic champion. She has proved herself to be single-minded and focused in everything that she has achieved, but has always remained calm and kept a smile on her face. Jessica has fans all over the world, who admire her ability and love the fact that she seems so down-to-earth and unaffected by the fame and money that have come with her sporting success.

Jessica Ennis crosses the finish line to win Olympic gold at the end of two days of demanding athletics events.

Jessica's father Vinnie was born in Jamaica but moved to England, where he settled in Sheffield and worked as a painter and decorator. He married Jessica's mother Alison, a social worker, and they had two daughters: Jessica and Carmel.

Jessica first went to an athletics stadium as a child aged 10 in the summer of 1996. She and her sister Carmel had been arguing a lot, so their parents sent them to a summer athletics camp at the Don Valley Stadium in Sheffield to see if they enjoyed the sport. Jessica appeared to have some natural athletic ability. She says of this experience: "It was the first time I ever experienced proper sport and it changed my whole life ... I'm grateful my parents were so fed up with us that they shipped us off there, because it changed everything."

Jessica was skilled at the **hurdles**, and soon after she was trying out a multi-event sport called the heptathlon. Jessica started to train regularly at Sheffield Athletics Club. When she was 13 years old, she met her current coach, Toni Minichiello. He was able to spot her potential early on and he has coached Jessica throughout her amazing athletics career.

WHAT IS THE HEPTATHLON?

The women's heptathlon is a gruelling two-day event during which athletes compete in seven different sports. The sports in the heptathlon are 100-metre hurdles, long jump, high jump, shot put, javelin, 200 metres, and 800 metres. Heptathletes need to have an excellent combination of athletic attributes including strength, stamina, and speed. Points are awarded to the competitors after each of the seven events. The highest score ever achieved in a heptathlon is 7,291. This record was set at the 1988 Seoul Olympics in South Korea by the legendary athlete Jackie Joyner-Kersee.

MONDO 🏃🏃🏃🏃 Sherbrooke 2003

Jessica leaps over a hurdle while competing at the 2003 World Youth Championships in Canada.

Jessica lived with her family in the Highfield area of Sheffield and attended King Ecgbert School. She worked hard at school and achieved good exam results, so she was able to carry on and study for her A levels. After finishing school, Jessica went to university to continue her studies. She studied psychology and worked hard to gain her degree. She graduated from the University of Sheffield in 2007 and began to concentrate on her athletics career.

During her time at school and university, Jessica was always busy training hard and competing at various athletics meetings around Great Britain and the world. Her first success came at the age of 14, when she won a schools high jump competition. Her performance was so impressive that she won a special prize, called the Whitham Award. This award is presented by the Sheffield Federation of School Sports in recognition of the best performance by a young Sheffield athlete.

Jessica clears the high jump bar during the World Junior Championships in Italy in 2004.

International debut

Jessica showed great potential and gave some impressive early performances, including first place in the heptathlon at the European Junior Championships and finishing eighth in the World Junior Championships. In 2006, Jessica made her debut at a major international athletics event at the Commonwealth Games in Melbourne, Australia. She performed brilliantly, achieving a new personal best total score after the two-day heptathlon competition, and winning a bronze medal for finishing third. This was an excellent way for Jessica to begin her international athletics career as an adult, and was the start of a period of constant improvement and better results.

In 2007, Jessica competed at her first World Championships, a competition second only to the Olympics in terms of **prestige**. The 2007 games took place in Osaka, Japan, and Jessica finished in fourth position. She missed out on a medal, but did set a new personal best total score of 6,469 points. This was a very credible result alongside a group of experienced heptathletes from all over the world.

Jessica's continued improvement at this time was noticed by more and more people, and in September 2007 her performances were rewarded with the first ever European Athletics Rising Star award. The winner of this award is chosen by athletics fans, the **media**, representatives from the European Athletics Member Federations, and an expert panel. Jessica was the first female winner of this prestigious award, which was presented to promising French sprinter Christophe Lemaitre in 2009 and Olympic discus gold medallist Sandra Perković in 2010.

Jessica finished fourth in her first ever World Championship heptathlon.

Jessica receives advice and encouragement from her long-time coach, Toni Minichiello, during a competition.

JESSICA'S COACH

Toni Minichiello has been helping Jessica train and compete since she was 13 years old. As her coach, he has seen her grow from a young girl into an extremely focused and successful woman. From the start it was clear to Minichiello that Jessica has many of the attributes that make a successful athlete. Along with her natural athletic ability, she is also intelligent and willing to learn. Minichiello has been alongside Jessica through all her triumphs at major athletics championships around the world. He has also been with her when things have not been going so well, such as times when she has been injured.

Entering 2008, Jessica's life was looking great. She was still learning and taking the advice of her coaches, and her heptathlon results were becoming more consistent. She was very much looking forward to competing at her first Olympics in Beijing, China, in the summer.

The injury

The injury that forced Jessica out of the Beijing Olympics was a **stress fracture** to her foot. The news that Jessica would not make it to the Olympics was devastating for her and all her fans. Jessica later said, "I was told by the UK Athletics doctor that this was a career-threatening injury. At that point my heart absolutely sank and I was worrying that it would be the end of my career at the age of 22."

The disappointment of missing her first Olympic Games was massive, while the fear that her career might be over before she could truly show her full potential was very upsetting. Jessica was determined to put the upset behind her and focus on getting back to full fitness, ready to take on the world again in her chosen sport as soon as she could. In a typically positive and brave way, she told the world's press: "I am determined to make a full and speedy recovery and enjoy a long athletics career."

The recovery

It took time for Jessica to regain full fitness and she needed to rest before she could compete again. She also had to cope with the distress of not competing. She found this time very difficult to cope with. During her recovery, Jessica spent six weeks on crutches. She was unable to drive and had to rely on her family and her coaches to help her get around.

When her foot was beginning to heal, Jessica started to jog in a pool to help strengthen it. After four months, her foot had healed and she was able to start training again.

Disaster strikes for Jessica when she injures her foot while competing in 2008, dashing her Olympic hopes.

Jessica is overjoyed with her gold-medal-winning result at the 2009 World Championships in Berlin.

The IAAF World Championships in athletics take place every two years. The World Championships event is smaller in size than the Olympic Games, with fewer competitors and events.

After fully recovering from her stress fracture, Jessica continued where she had left off before the disappointment of injury and missing the Beijing Olympics. Her level of performance and results steadily returned to the stage she was at before the injury. This meant that in 2009 she was fit and ready to take on the rest of the world in the heptathlon at the World Championships in Berlin, Germany.

First gold

Jessica entered the competition as the favourite to win the gold medal. But she was competing against the top heptathletes in the world and had the added pressure of being the favourite.

After the opening day's events, Jessica was in first position. She won the 100-metre hurdles, high jump, and 200 metres, and also recorded a new personal best distance in the shot put. The second day was more difficult for Jessica, as she only managed to finish ninth in the long jump and tenth in her weakest event, the javelin. In the final event of the 800 metres, she fought hard for the fourth quickest time, which meant that her total score was better than any of her competitors. Jessica became World Champion and set a new personal best total score of 6,731. Jessica had overcome any doubts that she or anyone else might have had about her temperament or her ability to cope with pressure and expectation.

Jessica continued her success on the track and field over the next two years, winning the gold medal in the heptathlon at the 2010 **European Championships** with a new personal best total score. She followed this by finishing as runner-up at the World Championships in 2011. By this time, Jessica had become a very recognizable face in Britain and around the world. Her success and fame led to many companies approaching Jessica to ask her to help promote their products.

Athletes do not earn very much money from competing, but they can add to their earnings with **sponsorship** deals and advertising contracts. Very good athletes with a proven success record, such as Jessica, can attract the interest of major global companies. Before the London 2012 Olympics began, Jessica was reported to be earning as much as £1 million from advertising.

Earning potential

Jessica currently has contracts with huge companies such as adidas, Coca-Cola, and British Airways. They use her image to promote their products because she is a great ambassador for sport and she is so recognizable. Jessica is loved by many fans around the world, and so is the perfect person to use in advertising campaigns. Jessica's contract with adidas is reportedly worth over £300,000 a year and she promotes their products worldwide.

Jessica showing off her British team adidas kit before the Olympics.

Charity work

As well as increasing her bank balance, Jessica has used her success and fame to help people less fortunate than herself. Jessica is passionate about doing work for charity and she is closely linked with The Children's Hospital Charity, Wells Sports Foundation, and a local cancer charity in Sheffield. Her work with Wells Sports Foundation includes working in schools with young people, helping to inspire them.

Jessica talks with young children who are interested in becoming athletes at the English Institute of Sport in Sheffield.

There was a long build up to the 2012 Olympic Games in London. The city had been chosen in 2005 as host for the 2012 summer games. In the years leading up to the competition, lots of money was spent on creating a new athletics stadium, as well as other new venues for sport including a **velodrome** and **aquatics centre**. This was also a time of anticipation and anxiety for the organizers and British athletes who would be taking part. There was excitement about hosting such an incredible event in London, but also concerns that the Games would not run smoothly, or that the British athletes would struggle to match the haul of medals won at recent Olympic Games.

Many people referred to Jessica as "the Face of the Games" because her image was so widely used. She played a huge part in the promotion of the London 2012 Games. Jessica's is a very recognizable face in Britain and her image seemed to be on everything from posters to boxes of washing powder! An image of Jessica in red, white, and blue kit 52.7 metres (173 feet) high was painted on to a field near Heathrow Airport with the words: "Welcome to our turf."

This was an exciting time for Jessica, but also added to the pressure she was already feeling as she waited to compete at her first ever Olympic Games.

THE OLYMPIC GAMES

The Olympic Games are the most famous athletics championships in the world. This highly prestigious event is held every four years in a different country. The most recent Olympic Games were held in London, England, in 2012 and the next will take place in Rio de Janeiro, Brazil, in 2016. The Olympics bring together more than 10,000 athletes from all over the world to compete in a total of 26 different sports. Winning a medal at the Olympics is a massive achievement, and winning a gold medal can change an athlete's life.

Jessica was the "Face of the Games" for London 2012, her image appearing on posters and adverts all over Great Britain.

The night of Saturday 4 August 2012 will always be remembered by British athletics fans. In the space of just one hour, three British athletes won gold medals in front of a capacity crowd of 80,000 people in the Olympic Stadium. The night that created so many headlines became known as "Super Saturday" and anyone who witnessed it would remember it for a very long time.

A thoroughly deserved win

Jessica had already produced some fantastic performances on the Friday, the first day of the heptathlon. She created a huge amount of excitement by winning the opening event, the 100-metre hurdles, smashing the British record in the event. Jessica followed this up with good, consistent results in the remaining events and led overall after day one. By the end of the second day of competition, Jessica had won the gold medal by more than 300 points and set a new British record in the heptathlon. She had won two of the events outright, come joint first in the 200 metres, finished runner-up in the long jump, and managed to execute two good throws in her weakest events, the shot put and javelin. The final event, the 800 metres, was a comfortable win for Jessica. After all the pressure leading up to the Olympics, she was able to enjoy her final event and celebrate her success.

JESSICA'S LONDON 2012 PERFORMANCE

Event	Result
100-metre hurdles	1st place, 12.54 seconds
High jump	5th place, 1.86 metres
Shot put	joint 9th place, 14.28 metres
200 metres	joint 1st place, 22.83 seconds
Long jump	2nd place, 6.48 metres
Javelin	10th place, 47.49 metres
800 metres	1st place, 2.0865 seconds

World-class athlete

Jessica proved that she is a truly world-class athlete and has a great future ahead. Four-time gold medal winner and athletics commentator Michael Johnson said of Jessica's success, "This is a phenomenal performance. After suffering the disappointment of missing Beijing through injury she then comes back at a home Olympics to prove to everyone that she is the best. Not only that but that she can perform under incredible pressure and win gold."

Her proudest moment:
Jessica kisses her Olympic gold medal.

Immediately after winning the Olympic heptathlon, Jessica said, "It's been the longest two days of my life. I can't believe it. I am world champion, I feel like crying. I've dreamt so many times about winning medals and becoming world champion, doing a lap of honour. It's the best feeling in the world. I can't even put into words how I feel right now, it's such an adrenaline rush and such an amazing feeling."

Jessica and her fellow heptathletes celebrate together after the London 2012 Olympic heptathlon competition has finished.

1ST

Gold
Medal
Winner
Jessica Ennis
Athletics: Combined
Women's Heptathlon

Stamp of approval ... Jessica's success is printed on a stamp as part of the British Olympic celebrations.

Jessica's Olympic gold medal can now go alongside her World Championship and European Championship medals, as well as other awards that include an **MBE**, given to her in 2011. She also holds some impressive records. Shortly before the 2012 Olympics, Jessica finally broke the British heptathlon record that had stood for 12 years. The previous record-holder had been Denise Lewis, a former heptathlete and British athletics star.

Post-Olympic celebrations

As part of the celebrations following the London 2012 Games and as a symbol of their success, every British gold medal winner had their photo printed on a postage stamp. Along with this, the Post Office decided to celebrate the nation's pride in each of these athletes by having a traditional red postbox in their home town painted gold. The gold postbox that represents Jessica's triumph is in Sheffield city centre.

REAPING THE REWARDS

The hard work and dedication that Jessica showed in the years leading up to her success at the London 2012 Olympics certainly paid off. The gold medal that she is proud to show off is proof of that. Athletes have to make many sacrifices during their career because so much of their time is taken up with training. Many miss out on time spent with family and friends. It is a tough choice for athletes to distance themselves in this way. They do it so that they can reach the targets set by their coaches and achieve their goals. Luckily, an athlete's family and friends can be there to celebrate and enjoy moments of success together, and attend occasions when medals, awards, and prizes are given out.

Jessica and her proud parents after she received an MBE from Prince Charles at Buckingham Palace in 2011.

So many awards!

Following her Olympic success, Jessica was named as the 2012 winner of the women's European Athlete of the Year Award. The result came from a poll of fans, media, and an expert panel. The British public also voted for Jessica to be named British Olympic Athlete of the Year. In addition to this, she was nominated for the IAAF World Female Athlete of the Year and was runner-up for the BBC Sports Personality of the Year Award. For the BBC award she faced stiff competition from some of her London 2012 teammates, such as Mo Farah, tennis player Andy Murray, and cyclists Bradley Wiggins and Sir Chris Hoy. Jessica's outstanding performances deserve these awards, recognition, and respect.

Jessica was named "Olympian of the Year" in Cosmopolitan's Ultimate Woman of the Year Awards in October 2012.

WHAT NEXT?

After Jessica's amazing performance in 2012, she began to set new targets for her athletic career. There were many questions from her fans and the media, such as would she compete in the heptathlon at the Olympic Games in Rio de Janeiro in 2016? Or, would she concentrate on one particular discipline from the heptathlon? Her strongest individual event is the 100-metre hurdles, and she has already proved that her best time in the event is right up there with the top hurdlers in the world. Her breathtaking British record time in the 100-metre hurdles during the 2012 Olympic heptathlon showed that she is more than capable if she chooses this path.

Tired but happy ... Jessica lies down on the track following her win in the heptathlon at the London 2012 Olympics.

Jessica's future participation in athletics could change from competing in seven events to just one: the hurdles.

If Jessica decides to stay focused on the heptathlon, she will be hoping to emulate the great American heptathlete Jackie Joyner-Kersee by retaining her Olympic heptathlon crown. Jessica has certainly proved already that she has the talent and ability to succeed. She also has a great team of people around her to help her prepare and win in future competitions.

Bright future

Jessica seems to take everything in her stride. She appears to have no problems handling the fame, admiration, and pressure that come with being a top athlete and national hero. She seems perfectly comfortable being one of the most recognizable faces in Britain. Whatever Jessica decides to do next in athletics, she will undoubtedly make a success of it, and continue to excite and enthral her fans.

Timeline

1986   Jessica Ennis is born in Sheffield, Yorkshire.

1996   Jessica goes to the Don Valley Stadium to try athletics for the first time.

2000   Jessica wins the Whitham Award, presented by the Sheffield Federation of School Sports.

2005   Jessica wins a bronze medal at the World University Games, held in Turkey.

2006   Jessica wins the bronze medal at the Commonwealth Games in Melbourne, Australia.

2009   Jessica wins the World Championships gold medal in Berlin, Germany and sets a new personal best in the heptathlon.

Jessica is named Sportswoman of the Year by the British Sports Journalist Association (SJA).

2010   Jessica wins the gold medal at the European Championships in Barcelona, Spain.

2011   Jessica is awarded an MBE by Prince Charles.

Jessica wins a silver medal at the World Championships in Daegu, South Korea.

2012   Jessica breaks the British heptathlon record at a competition in Austria.

Jessica wins the gold medal at the London 2012 Olympics.

Jessica is named as female European Athlete of the Year.

Jessica is named as British Athlete of the Year.

2013   An Oxfam poll, celebrating International Women's Day, puts Jessica joint-first with the Queen as the most inspirational women in Britain.

Jessica marries her childhood sweetheart, Andy Hill.

Jessica lives with Andy Hill in Sheffield. The couple met at school and waited to get married until after the London Olympics, in 2013.

 Jessica owns a chocolate Labrador dog called Myla. She loves her very much.

 Jessica has held British records in the heptathlon, 100-metre hurdles, and high jump.

 Jessica likes to spend her spare time making lasagne!

 Jessica's favourite football team is Sheffield United, her local team.

 Jessica likes cake and sweets, and she keeps a bag of jelly sweets with a banana in her kit bag to provide an energy rush when it is needed.

 Jessica's sporting heroes are the former British heptathlete Denise Lewis and the former Swedish heptathlete Karolina Kluft.

 Jessica loves shopping – particularly for handbags!

JESSICA'S PERSONAL BESTS

Year	Personal best score in the heptathlon
2006	6,287
2009	6,731
2010	6,823
2012	6,955

GLOSSARY

aquatics centre arena for swimming and diving competitions

coach person who helps an athlete to train and win

Commonwealth Games international athletics competition held every four years, in which the 54 Commonwealth nations, including Great Britain, Canada, Australia, and India, compete

European Championships athletics event held every two years. Only athletes from European countries can take part in these championships.

heptathlon two-day athletics event in which athletes compete in seven different sports

hurdles track event where athletes leap over a series of upright frames

MBE Member of the Order of the British Empire. An honour given to someone by the Queen for a particular achievement.

media organizations that collect and broadcast news, in newspapers, on television, the internet, and radio

prestige respect given to something because it is important or of high quality

sacrifice give up something so that another good thing may happen

sponsorship agreement where an athlete is paid to promote certain products

stress fracture breaking of a bone or part of a bone caused by unusual or repeated stress

velodrome arena for indoor cycle racing. The arena contains a steeply banked oval track.

Books

Jessica Ennis, Roy Apps (Franklin Watts, 2012)

Olympic Champions, Nick Hunter (Wayland, 2011)

Olympic Stars, Laura Durman (Franklin Watts, 2011)

The London Olympics 2012, Nick Hunter (Raintree, 2011)

Websites

Aviva Startrack
http://academy.uka.org.uk/startrack/
Jessica Ennis started her athletics career with Aviva Startrack. Find out about sessions near you if you would like to take up athletics.

UK Athletics
http://www.uka.org.uk
Visit the UK Athletics website to find out about future athletics events and get news about British athletes.

London 2012
http://www.london2012.com
Find out more about the London 2012 Olympic Games on this website.

Disclaimer

All the Internet addresses (URLs) given in this book were valid at the time of going to press. However, due to the dynamic nature of the Internet, some addresses may have changed, or sites may have changed or ceased to exist since publication. While the author and Publishers regret any inconvenience this may cause readers, no responsibility for any such changes can be accepted by either the author or the Publishers. It is recommended that adults supervize children on the Internet.

INDEX